Abstract Colouring Book

Volume 1
Lines & Circles

by

June Krisko

Published by JK Creative Publishing in 2015
First edition; First printing

Illustrations and design © 2015 June Krisko

http://www.jkcreativepublishing.com

All rights reserved. No part of this book may be reproduced or transmitted in any form or by any means, including but not limited to information storage and retrieval systems, electronic, mechanical, photocopy, recording, etc. without written permission from the copyright holder.

ISBN   978-0-9949584-0-2

*I dedicate this book to my husband,
son and amazing friend Dawn.*

I love to feel in colour.

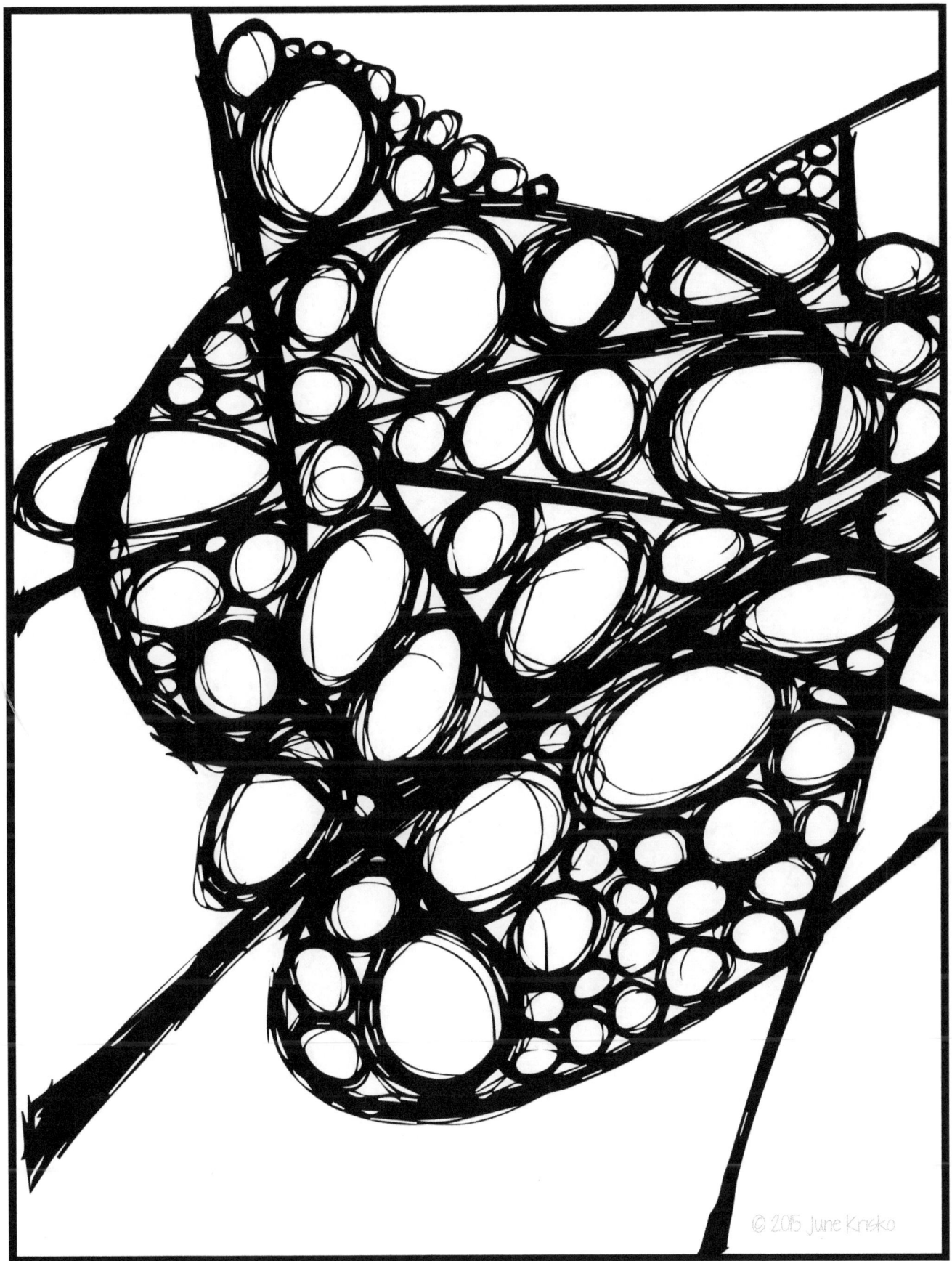

With yellow I can make the sun shine.

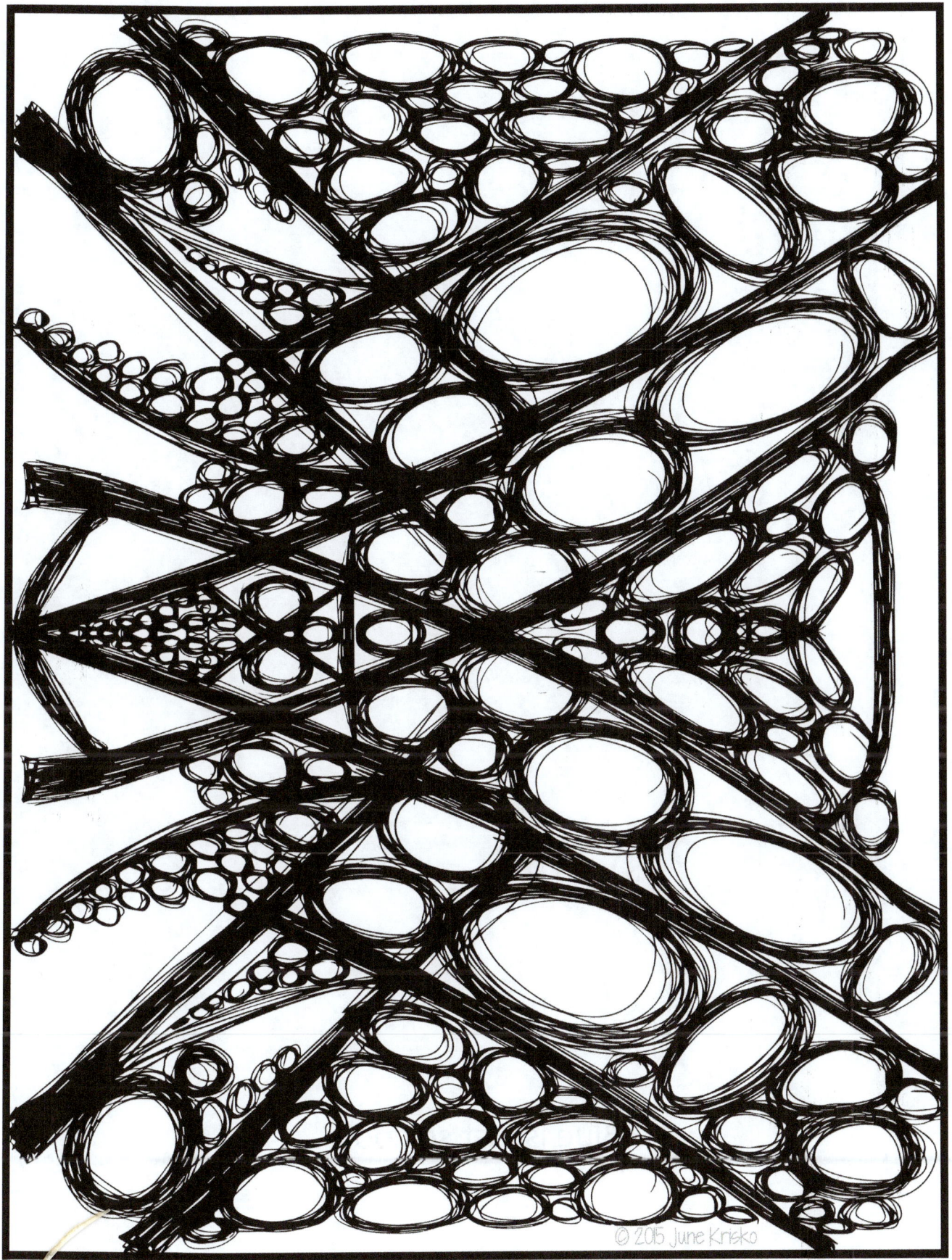

Blue is just so cool.

Purple makes my eyes dance.

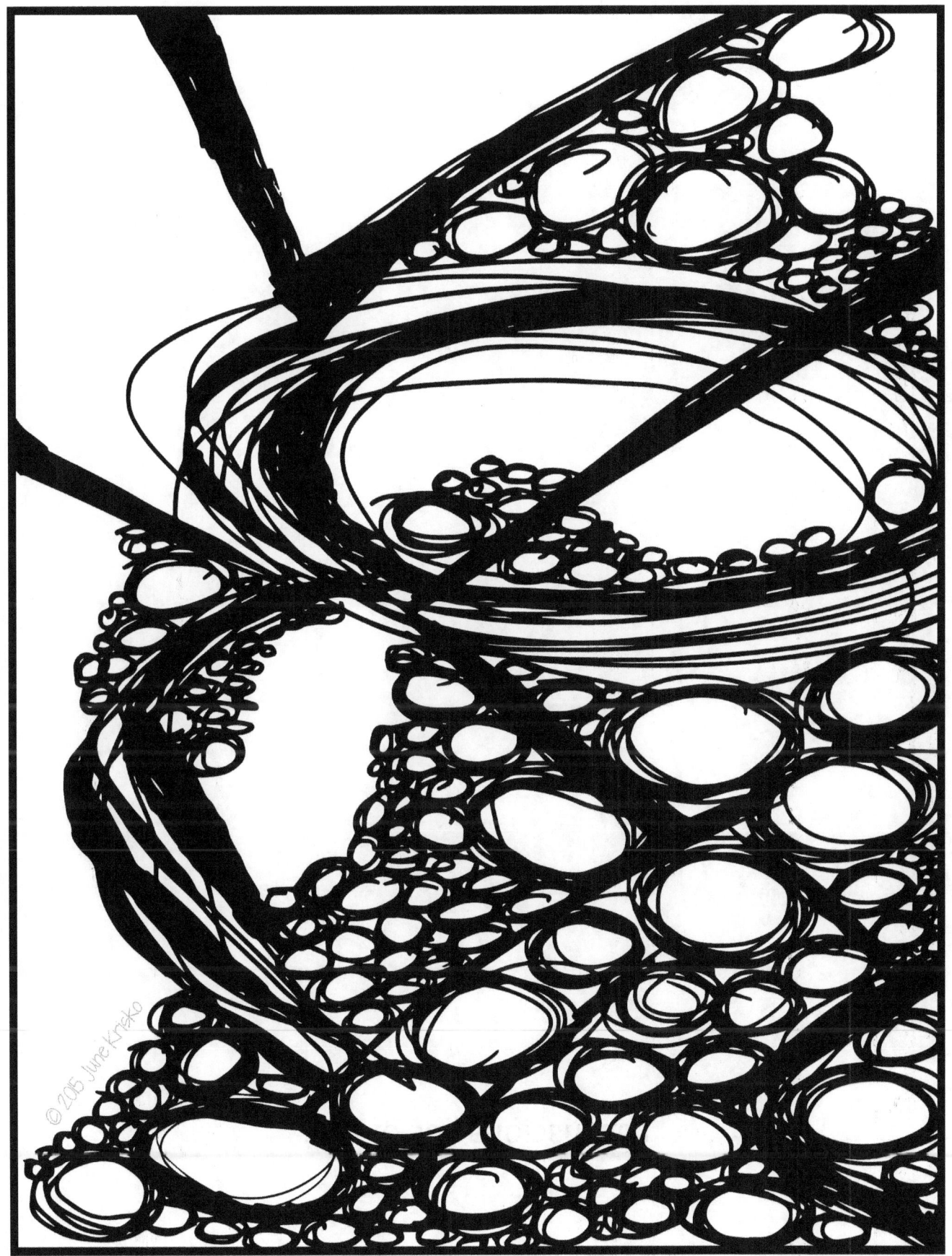

The luscious lips of red.

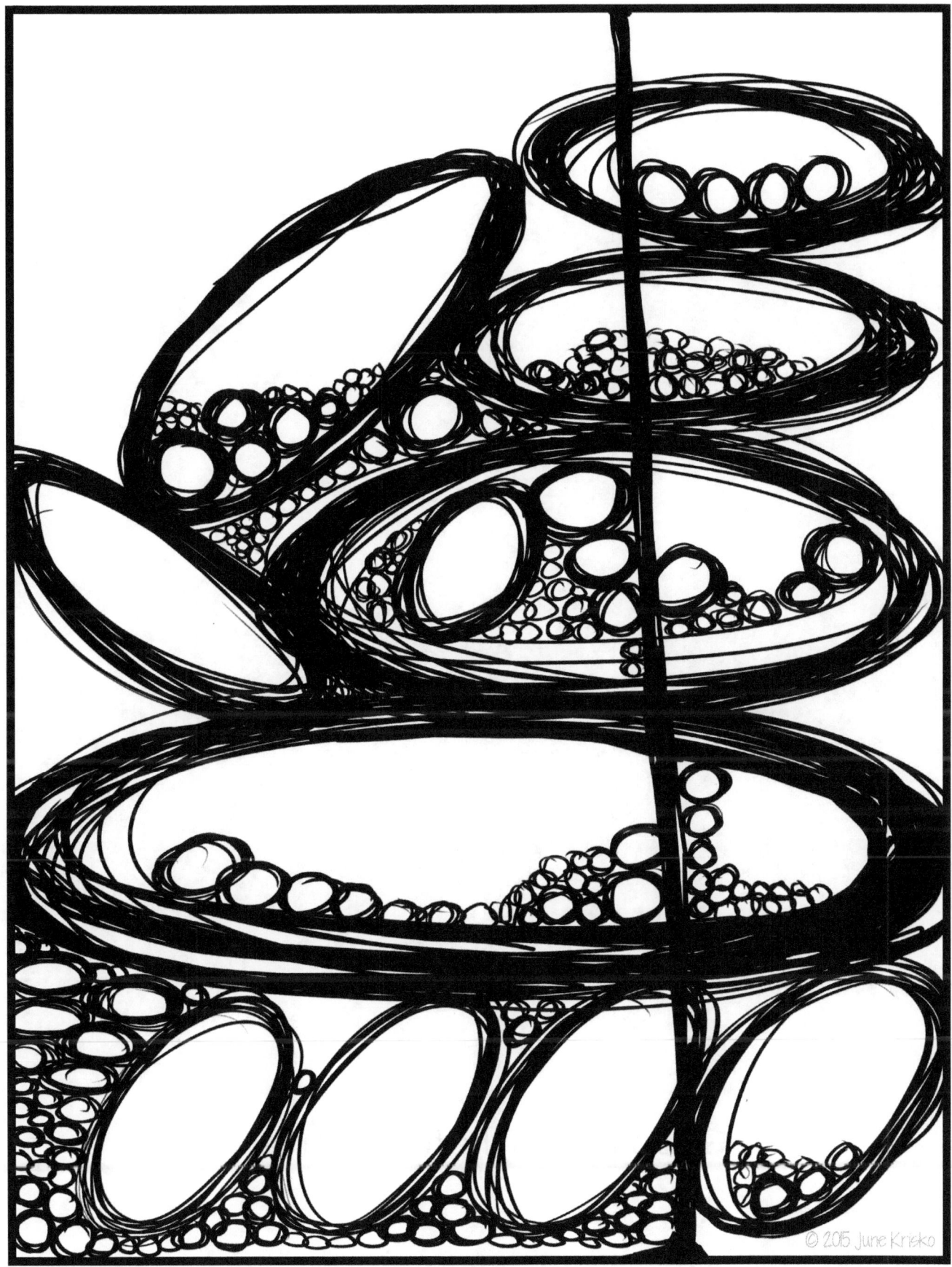

Getting lost in the field of green.

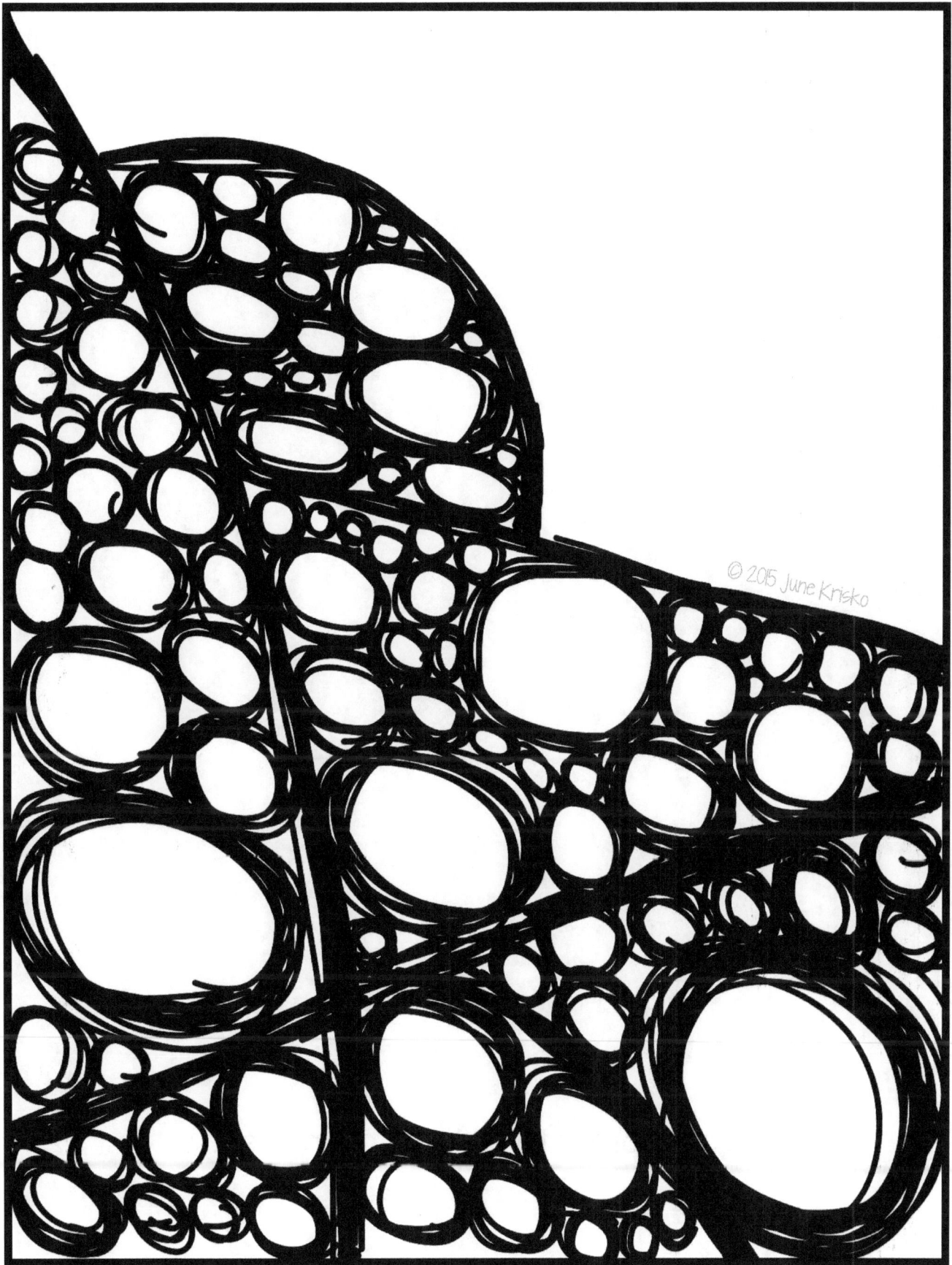

Don't forget to pick the cherry red.

Magenta warms my soul.

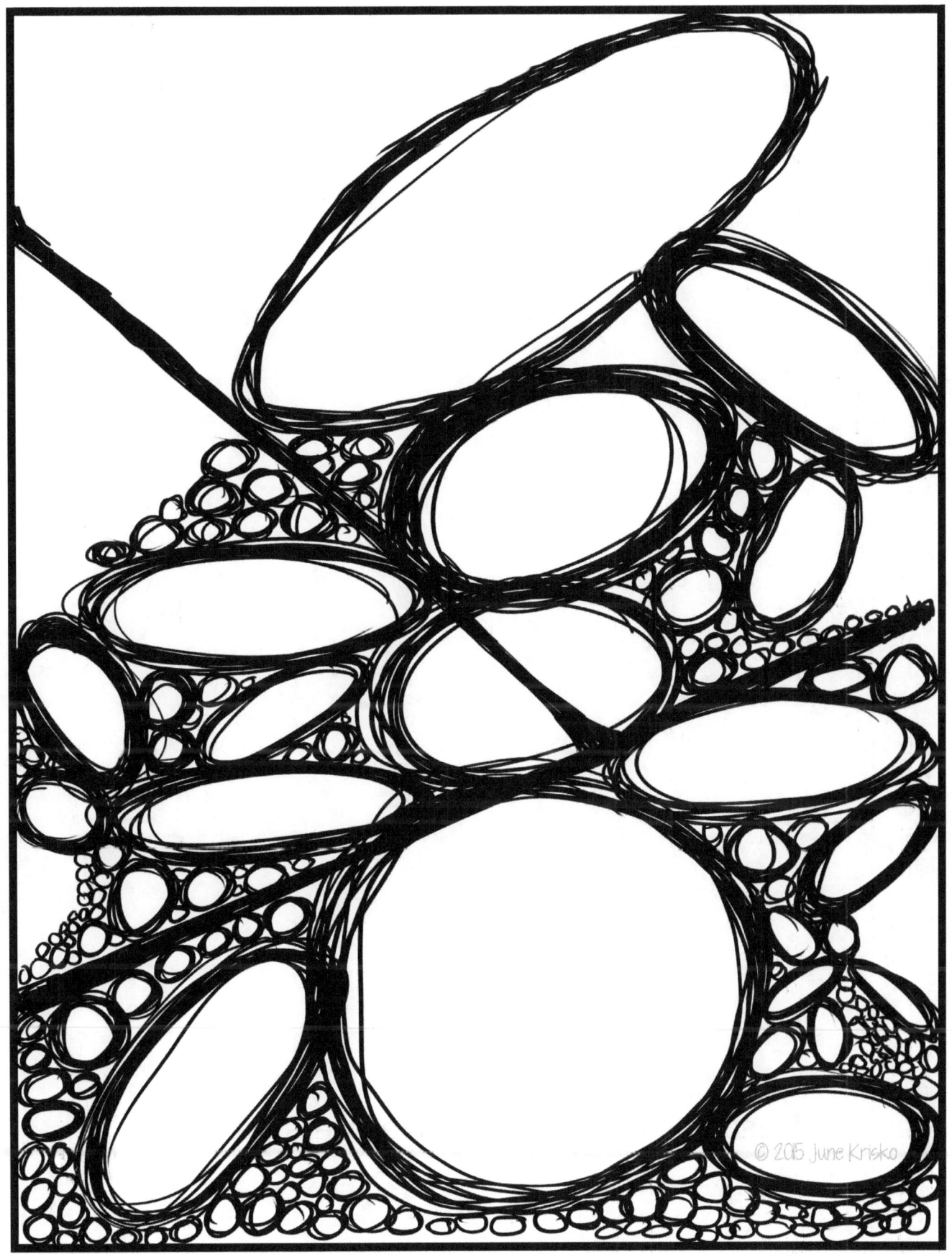

Need to start the day with espresso brown.

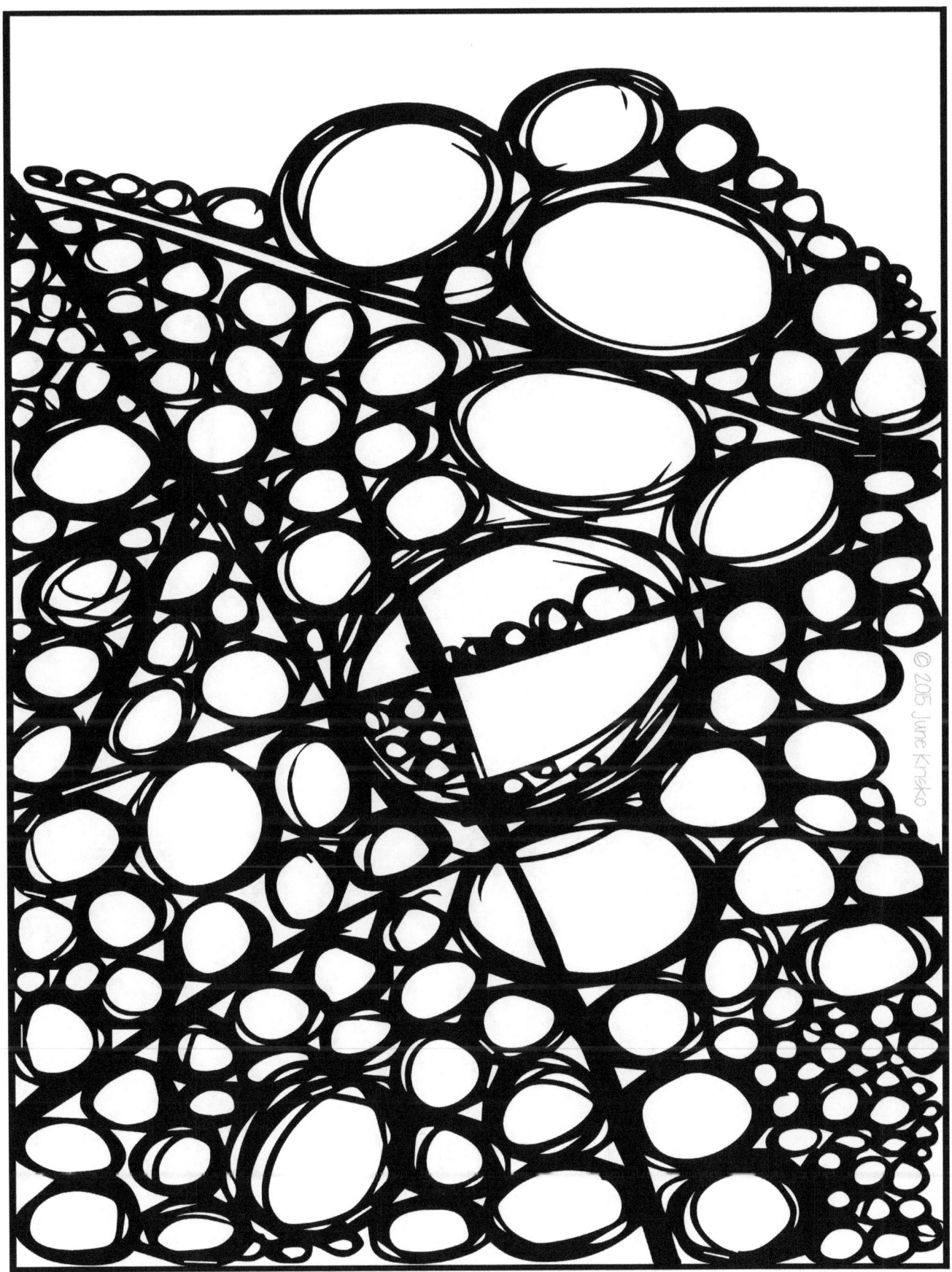

Pink is perfect.

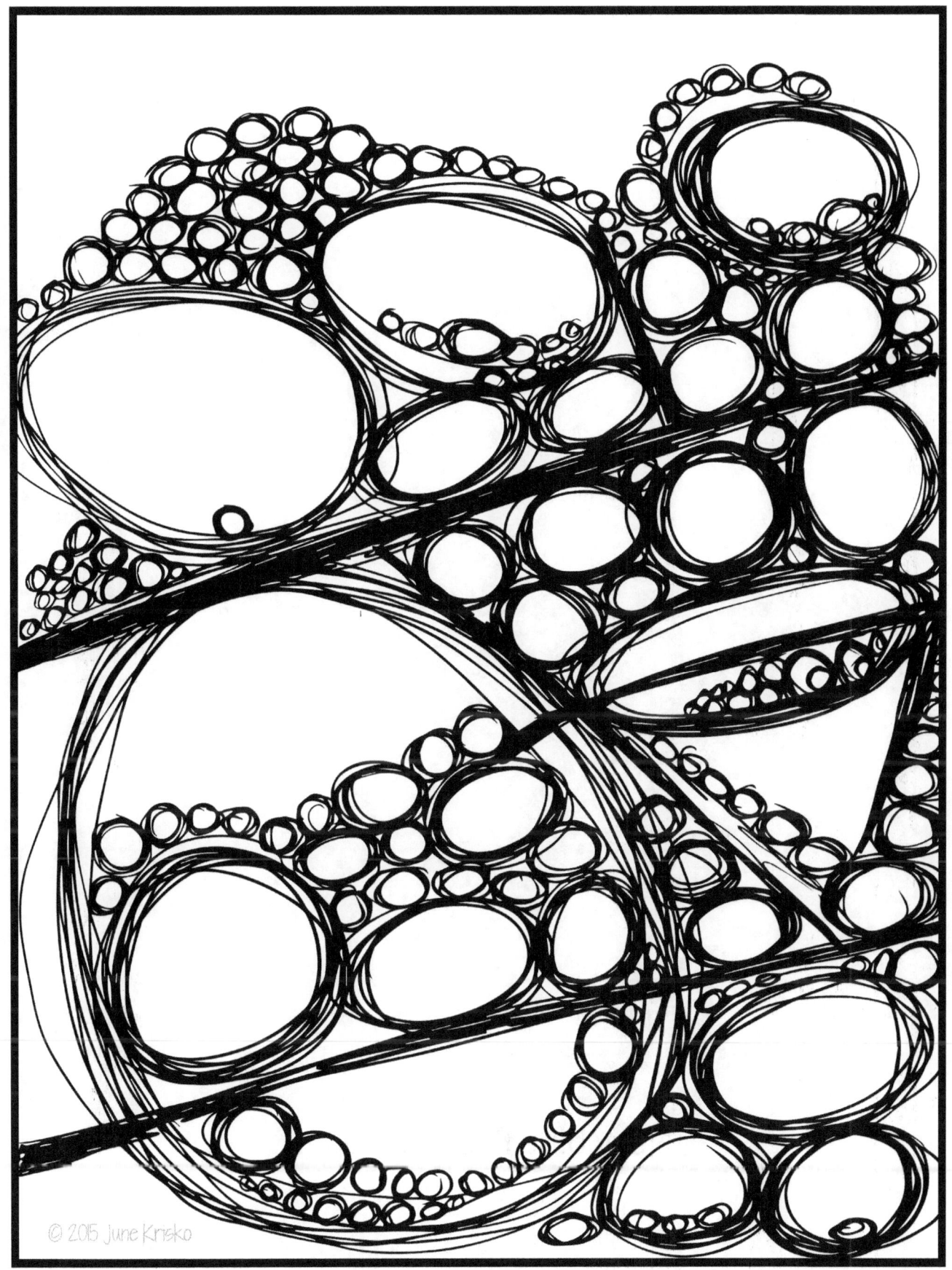

Navy blue floats my boat.

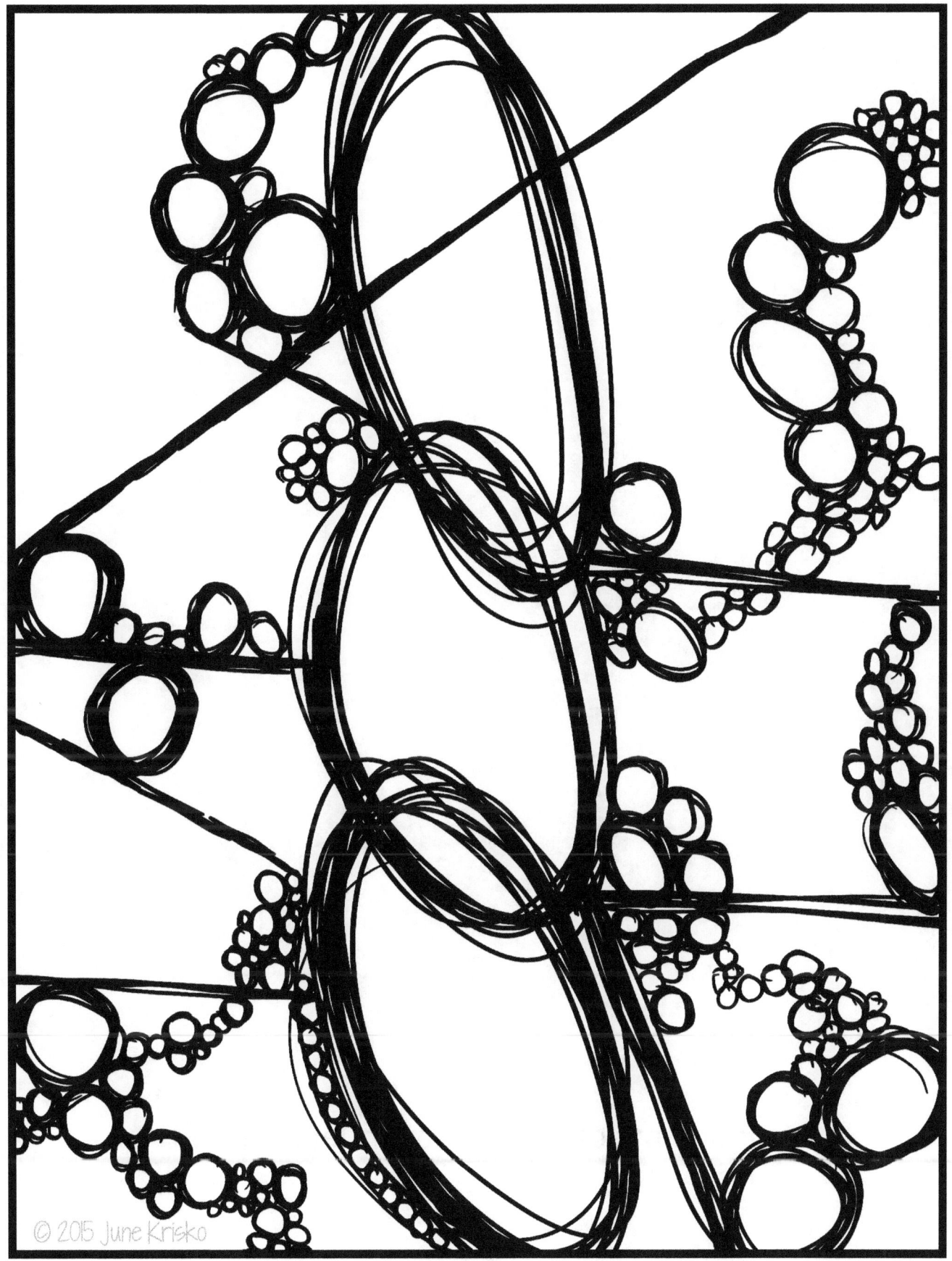

Calming my day with a lavender moment.

Peachy keen colours.

Grey is a shady character.

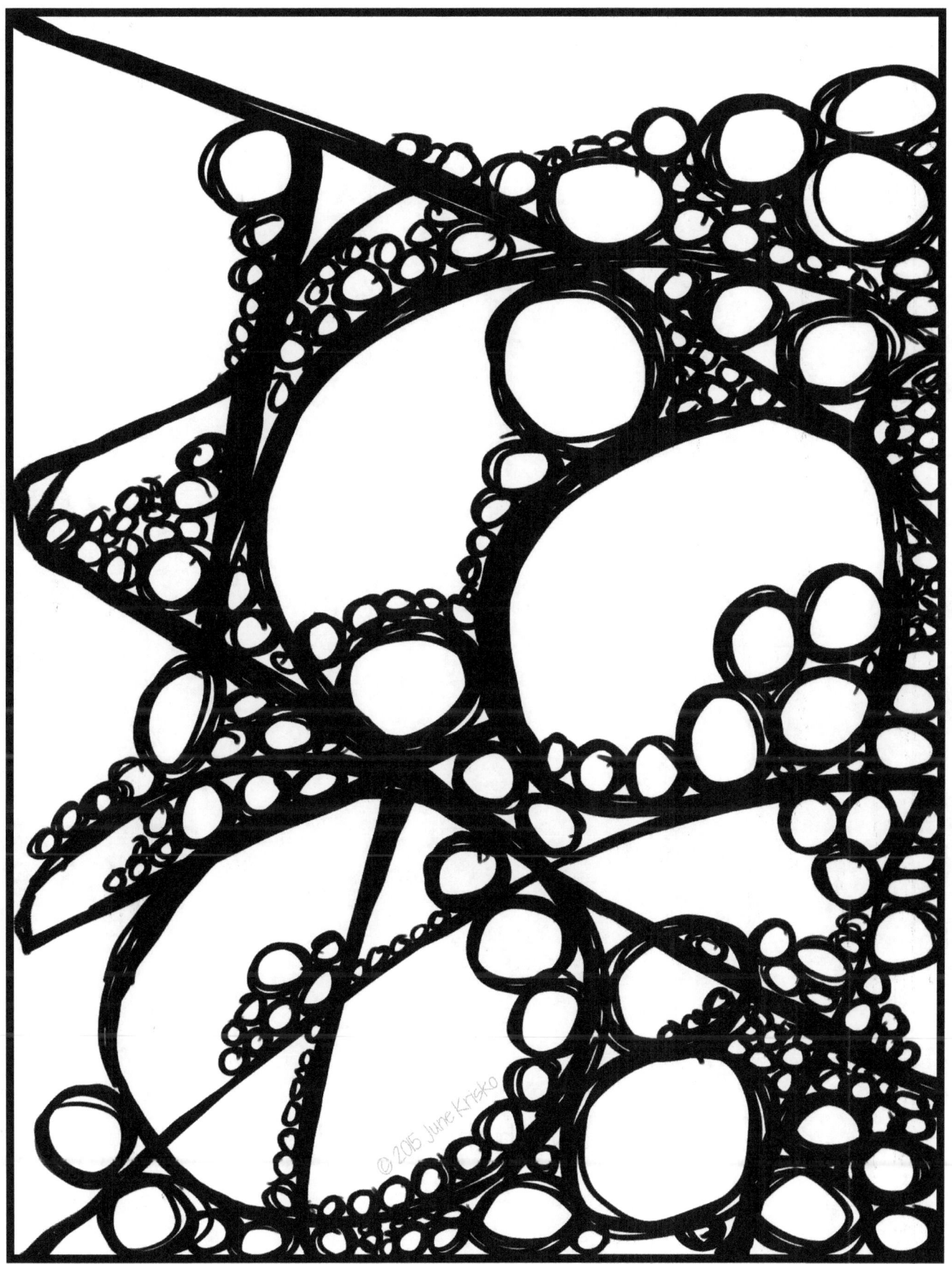

Playing with the baby blue.

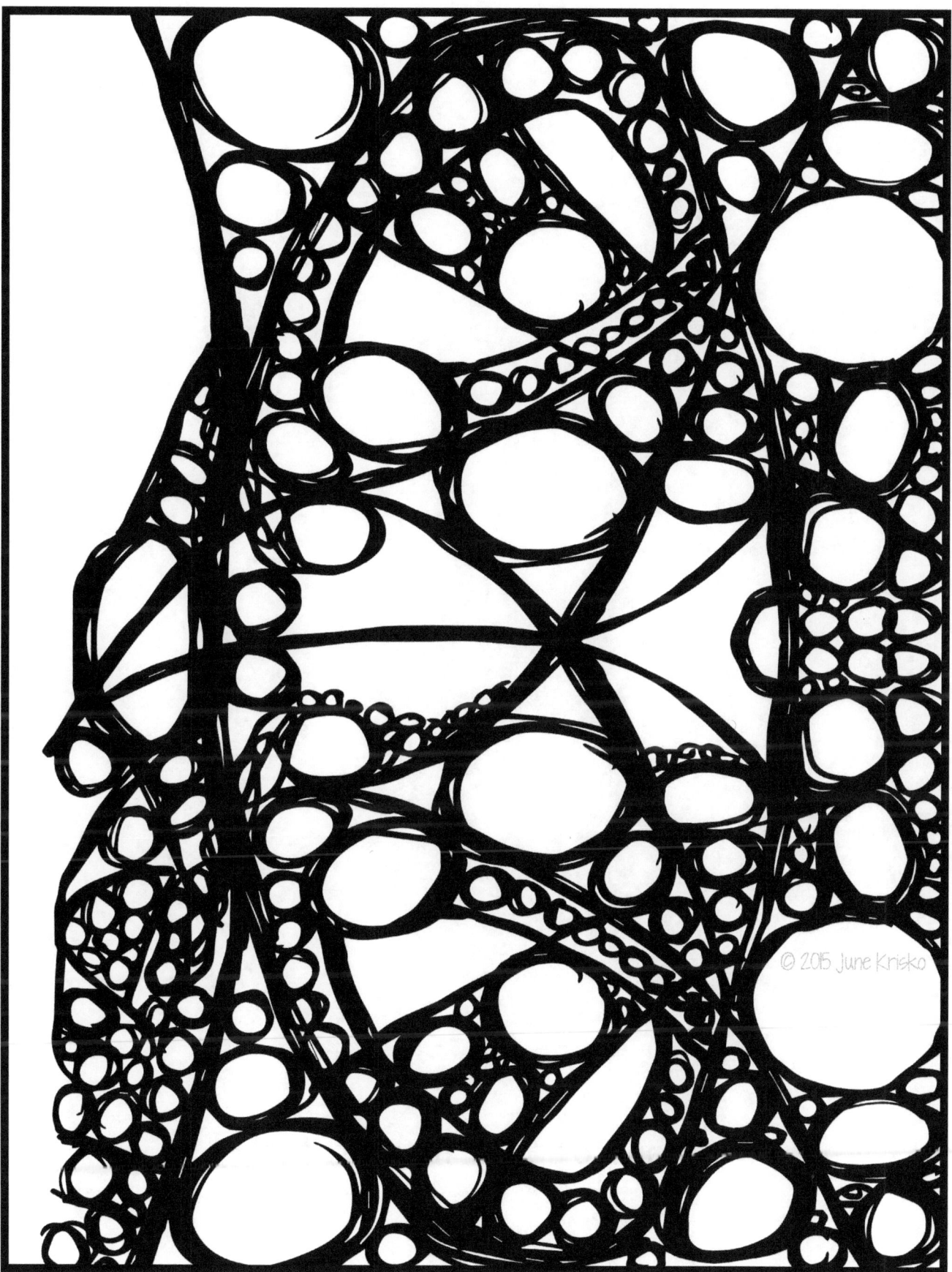

I want to appeal for more teal.

Turquoise is a special jewel in my pencil case.

Pale rose reminds me of a delicate flower.

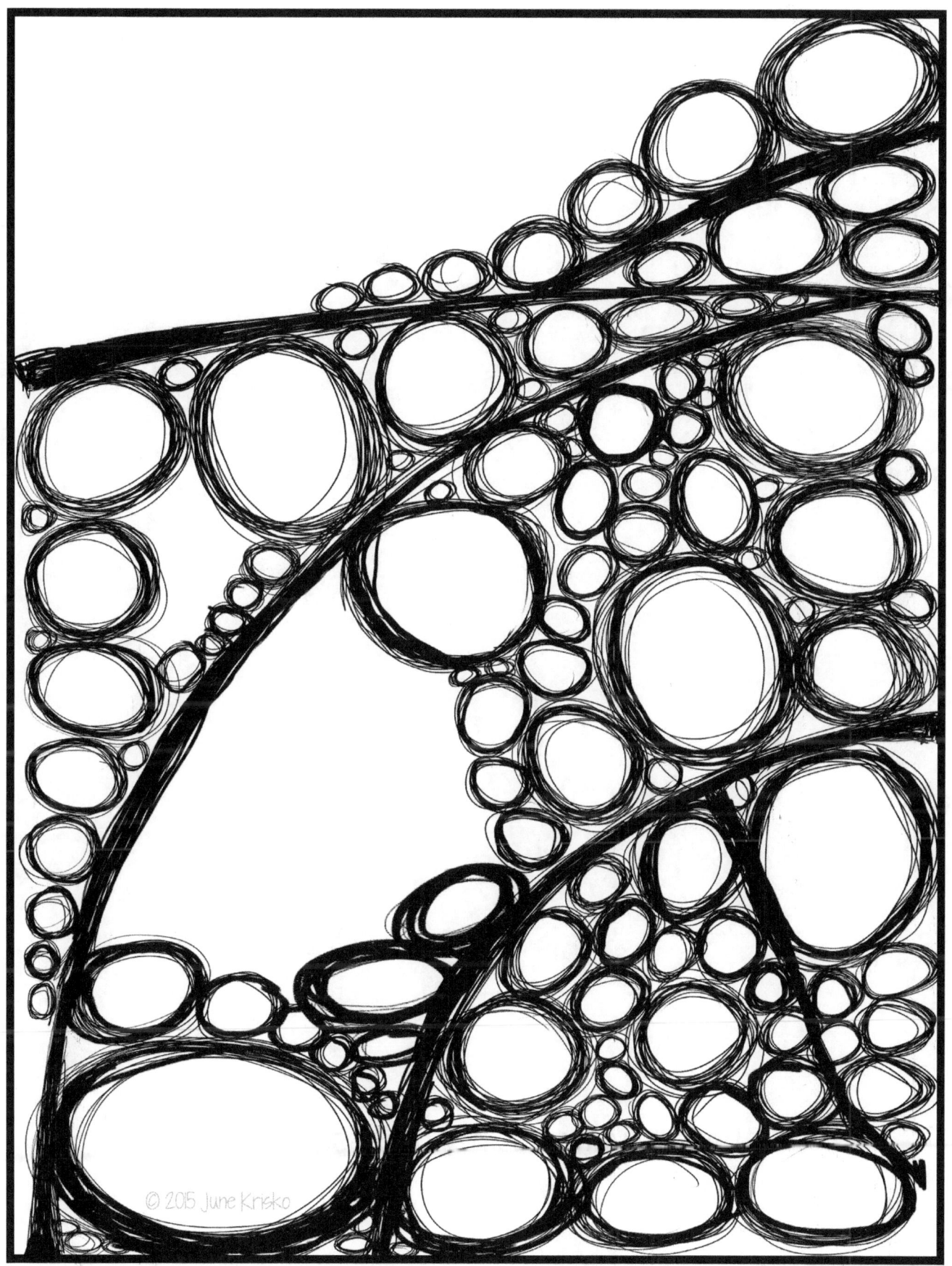

Lemon yellow is my main squeeze.

I find extra flavour in the minty green.

Aqua green brings a fresh perspective.

Pine green brings me to the forest floor.

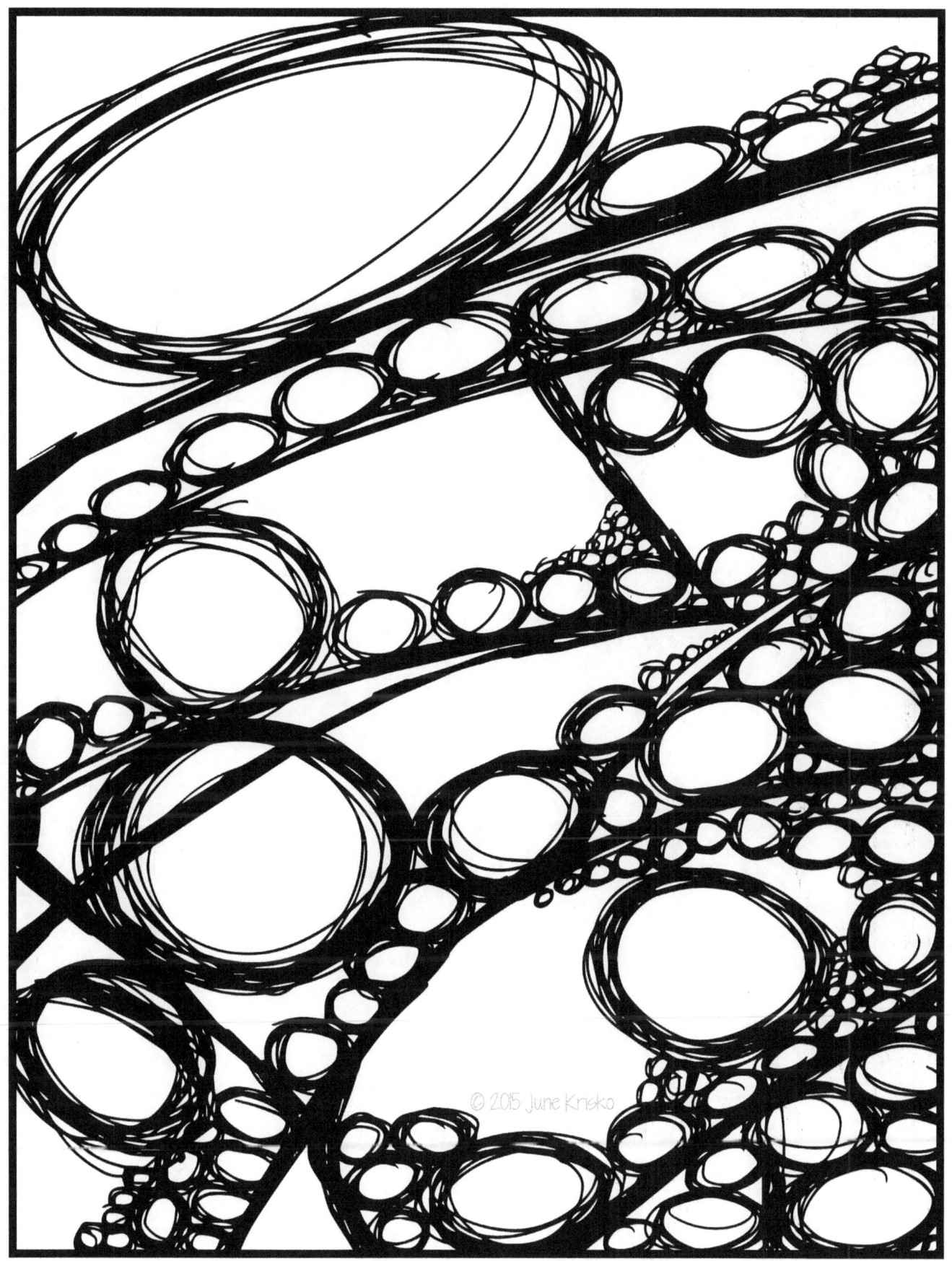

When I frown, I use dark brown.

Smooth as mahogany.

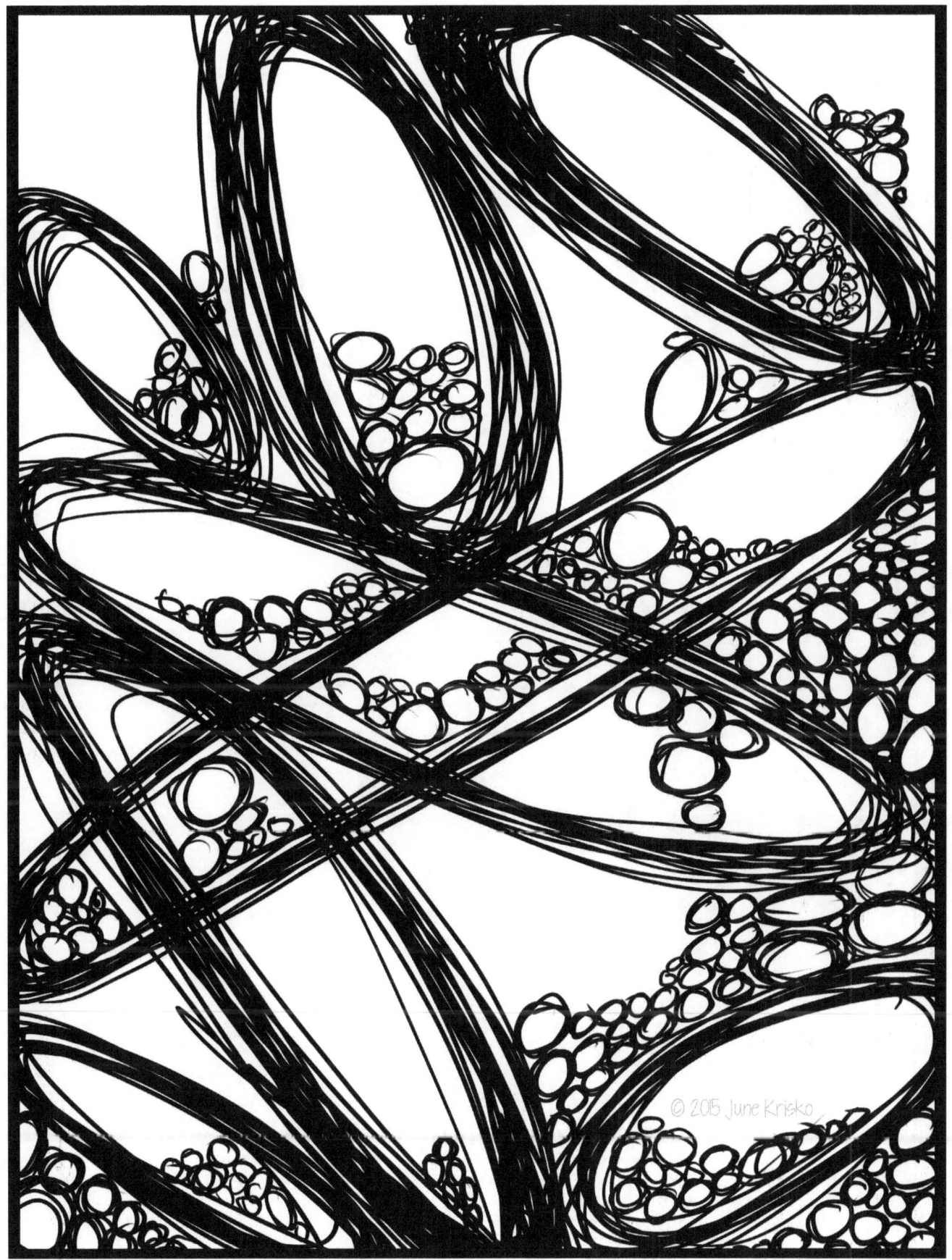

Crooning with my maroon.

Raspberry brings colour to my palette.

Pucker up for lime green.

Orange makes me feel healthy.

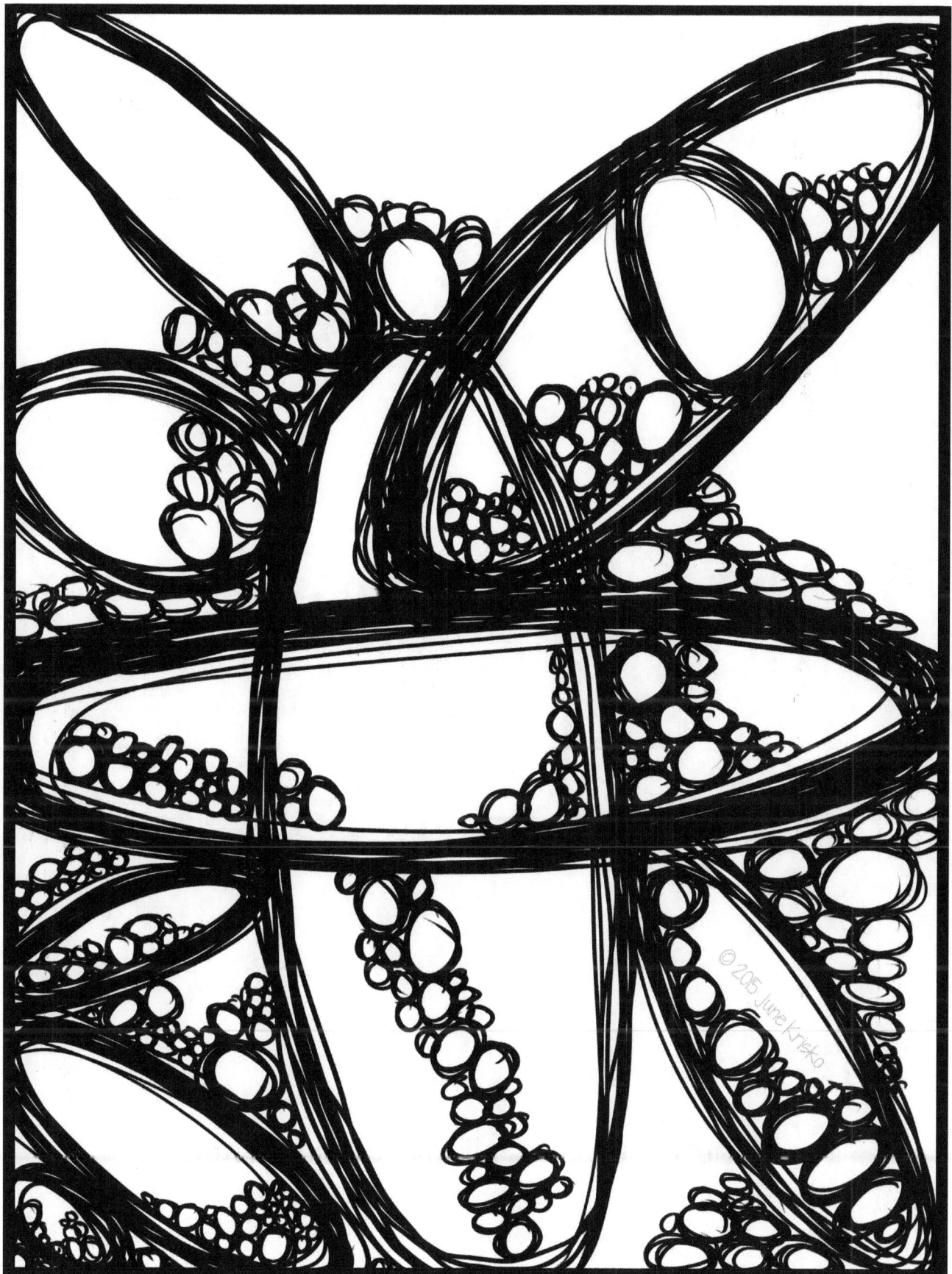

Amethyst makes all my colours richer.

Cerulean is a deep mystery for me.

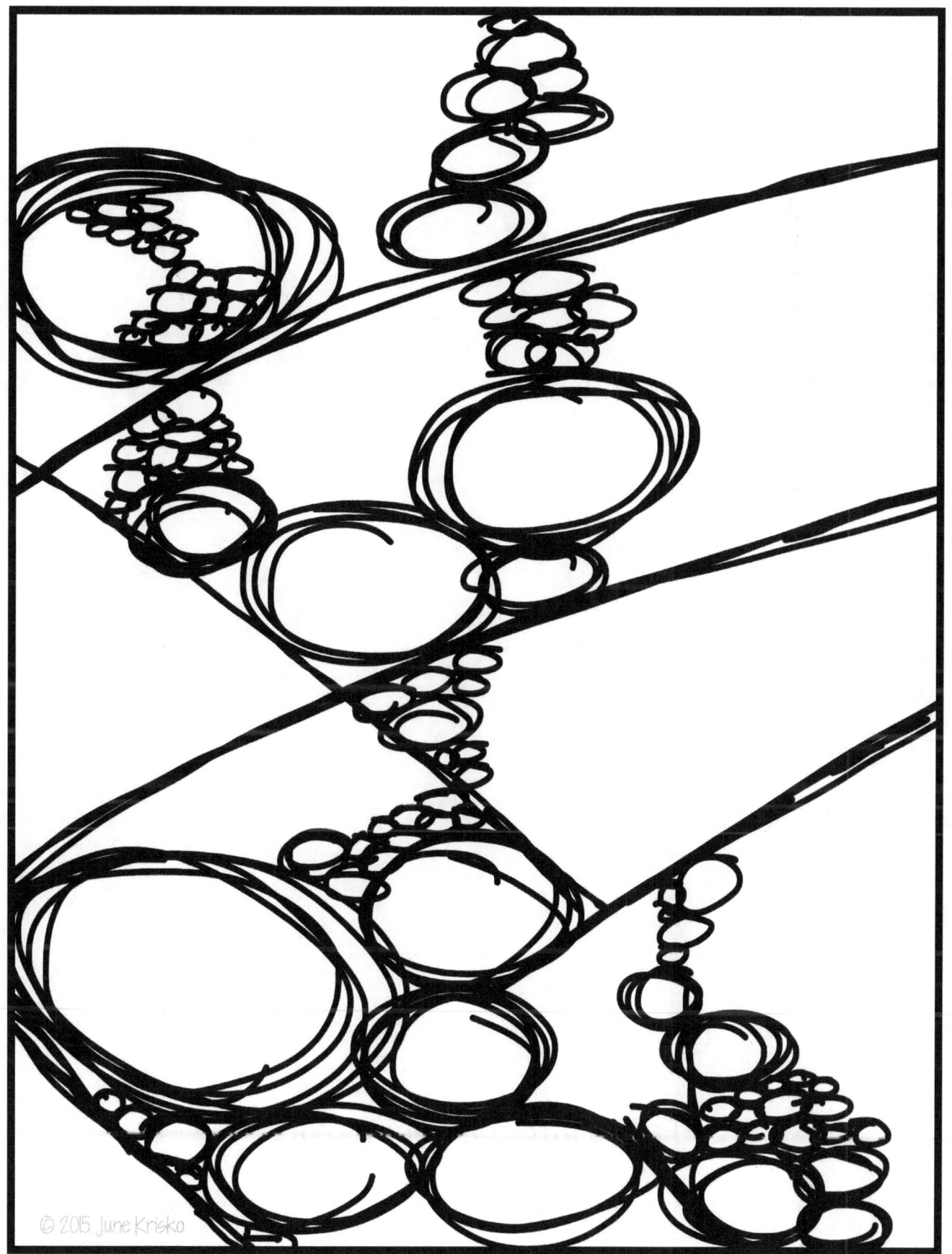

Faded into the denim blue.

Fruitful as the strawberry red.

The warm texture of tan.

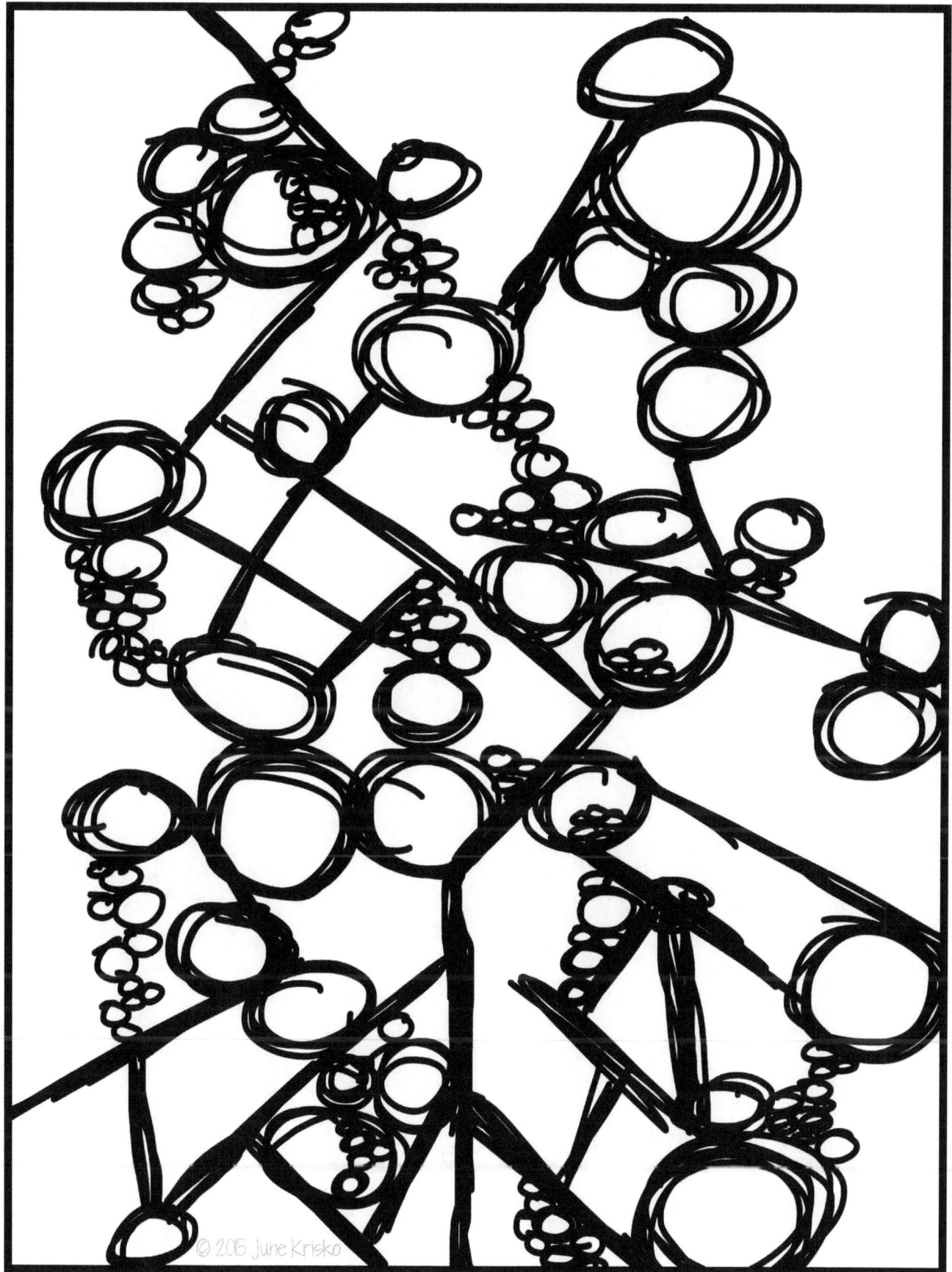

Tricked into jade green.

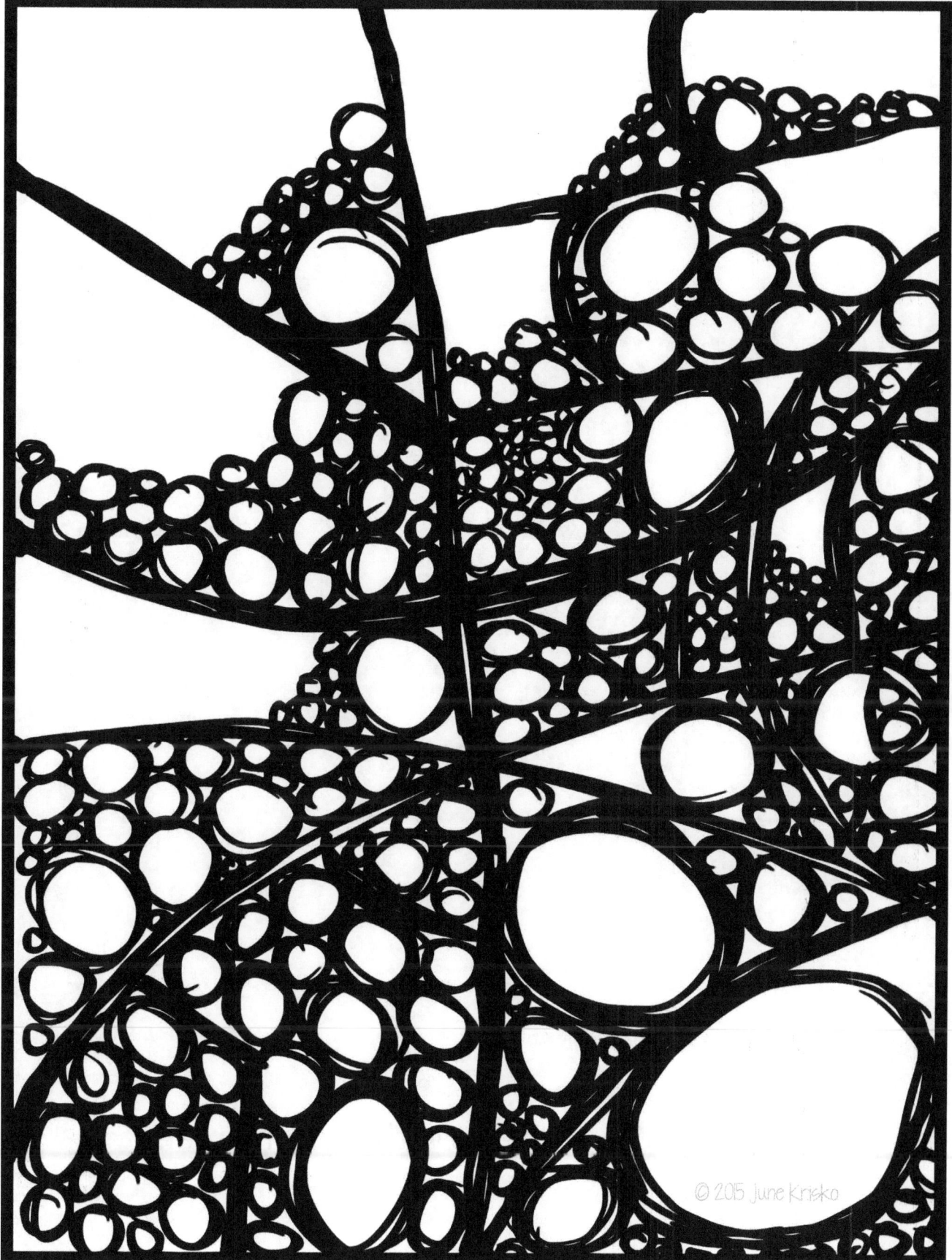

Feeling ocean breezes with my coral reef.

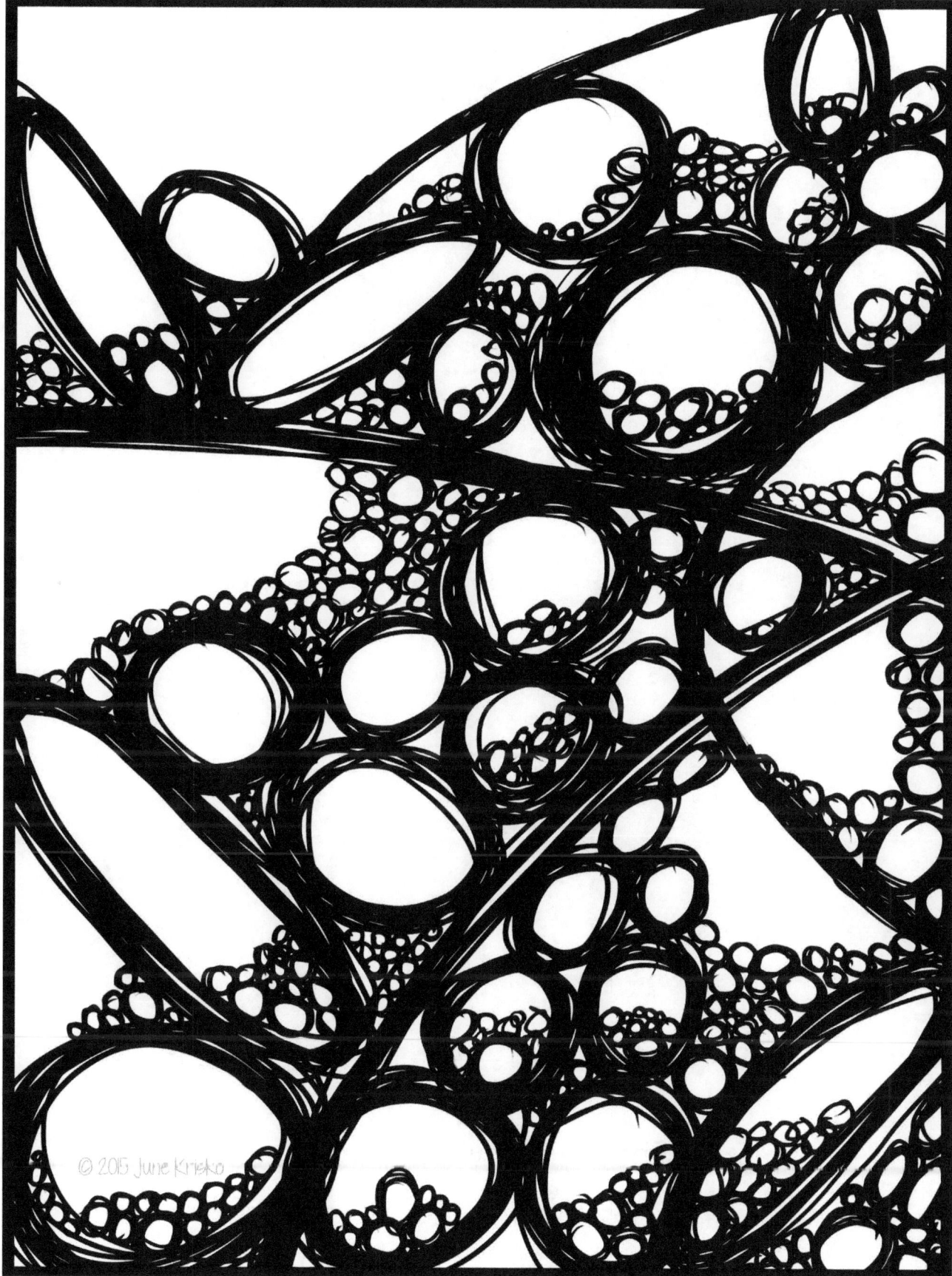

Shocked by violet purple.

I think of slate for my plate.

I have respect for royal blue.

I pound my fist for more copper.

Filling up the image with ocean green.

Coming soon...

Look for more
"Abstract Colouring Books"
and other types
of colouring books
online at
www.jkcreativepublishing.com.

June Krisko is a digital artist and photographer.

Born and raised in Canada, she studied Fine Arts at Redeemer College and Crafts & Design at Sheridan College.

She uses various digital techniques to create one-of-a-kind abstract works of art for publication.

www.ingramcontent.com/pod-product-compliance
Lightning Source LLC
Chambersburg PA
CBHW060457300426
44113CB00016B/2627